SOME NIGHTS NO CARS AT ALL

Josh Rathkamp

AUSABLE PRESS
2007

Cover art: "Street Lit Stroll"
Michael Bishop/Illustration Works/Getty Images

Design and composition by Ausable Press
The type is Perpetua with Perpetua Titling MT Light.
Cover design by Rebecca Soderholm
Author photo by Joanna Robbins

Published by
AUSABLE PRESS
1026 HURRICANE ROAD
KEENE, NY 12942
www.ausablepress.org

Distributed to the trade by
Consortium Book Sales & Distribution
1045 Westgate Drive
Saint Paul, MN 55114-1065
(651) 221-9035
(651) 221-0124 (fax)
(800) 283-3572 (orders)

The acknowledgments appear on page 89 and constititute a
continuation of the copyright page.

Library of Congress Cataloging-in-Publication Data

Rathkamp, Josh.
Some nights no cars at all / by Josh Rathkamp.—1st ed.
p. cm.
ISBN: 978-1-931337-35-9 (alk. paper)
I. Title.
PS3618.A87S66 2007
811'.6—DC22
2007025973

for my family

I

II

III

IV

In the slowness of time. Black time to white, & rind to blossom.
Deity is in the details & we are details among other details & we long to be

Teased out of ourselves. And become all of them.

—Larry Levis

I

AFTER A LONG SEPARATION

Although I promised nothing bad would happen,
the couch I pushed out our window
smashed the nest we watched
awaken each day with sparrows.

Picking it up I hoped
you wouldn't notice, just say one day
those noisy birds must have flown away.

I remember your glance
last winter, a witnessing, you said, as if
to witness was to see
three black birds on one white branch
the way a child does
running across the lawn after them.

And again I am finding ways
to clean the mess I made,
rationalizing their nest to fallen twigs
wound with mud and fishing line,
the simple possibility of making another.

EVERYONE WITH A SCAR
ON HIS CHIN

for B

Thinks he's alone.

Thinks that whatever happened
happened to make him
him.

Thinks that the crack
where the hair won't grow is a sign,

just as the cracks in his driveway,
the ones the shovel sticks in,
are a sign, a sign that says
cement grows.

And when he starts to forget
he's alone
the scar is there to remind him.

A new lover might ask
as she looks up
from his chest
and the story unfolds—

he says it starts with him thinking
he's alone.

THE FRENCHMAN

In Nice, you topless and me all golden,
we called ourselves *suavé* for a joke,
pronouncing it, while we drank red wine
from a bottle buried between our towels.

I kept looking around the beach
in fear that some flat-stomached Frenchman
sporting a Speedo,
although also a joke, would sweep you away.

And for a second the wind lifting the pink
dress you hold so gingerly against your thighs—

I am reminded that once you were naked
in public and unashamed. In fact,
I was more concerned for your breasts than you were,
repeatedly moving my body
to make shadow clouds above them.

OLDER GIRLS

Noah built a boat by hand.
Now that is a story

almost unbelievable at times
like these. Used to be

the two older girls
who walked across Frost Drive,

one lying down on my bed, the other
on my brother's, were real.

They would tell us they were sick
as we draped our yellow

plastic stethoscopes from our necks
and asked where it hurt.

One girl would point to her chest
and cough and smile, because

none of us knew
what innocence was yet.

I wanted to make good, even then,
lowering my ear to her breast,

listening for rain, which I know now
has everything to do with love.

SPECTATORS ALONG THE INTERSTATE

A few miles outside Kalamazoo we wonder
how on earth the first spring storm

blew the roof off a barn,
sent it dragging-ass like a barge out to sea.

On the news a farmer stood sure
of its connection to God; *it's representational,* he said,

as if the roof had perched on a church steeple.
By morning its picture plastered everywhere

brought people believing in miracles,
the roof in all its ridiculousness,

still erect, flown over the highway
in a perfectly flocked V. It's not hard to imagine

the spectators along the interstate,
the wet stuck smell of a wet corn field,

the roof, a big roof so sick of the years
of its body it had to let go, say yes to the wind,

yes to the water, yes to the earth that knows
the powerful and the beautiful have different names.

JUNE IN THE DESERT

Tonight relentless fires burn
an hour north of here.
At work we set out reamed boxes
of old paper to collect money
because there are so many
needy and how
can things be all right.

Last night my girlfriend said
that there wasn't a burning
between us, nothing that would make
her tape her life to mine,
but still we decide to wait
for something to grow
into something else.

How selfish it is to think
this way about fire,
about wanting it, about wishing
it could spread through the pines
with so much devastation
when it comes, it comes
big enough to burn us down.

THE BEGGAR'S CUP

In the darkness, you cup the desert cold
in my hand with your hand.
Even the dog, which is not ours,

tottering, arthritic, not really a dog
but a dog's shadow,
shivers where the path turns

away from the road. We follow it
like a flashlight. Only yesterday, it seems
you sprang into me.

While we walk you talk
explaining the inevitability of ourselves
meeting like this, on a path

of rocks. Tomorrow, you are leaving,
and New Hampshire
is nothing but leaf shade.

Still, who we are
is who we dreamed we'd be.
The days dangle off

dusty branches of a tree.
One gigantic cloud stops traffic, dead,
on the interstate. From here

if we drive out, shoulder to shoulder,
we'll become a little part of everything—
even that dark blue sky.

WHEN YOU WAKE, MICHIGAN IS STILL THREE HOURS AWAY

for Kate

I explain all the men in hunter's orange by saying *deer*.
Here, in this place, there is also a St. Louis,
cities divided by bridges, a season for blueberries.

Because you ask, I lay down miles of myself
in front of you. Soon, we will pass a fighter plane
propped on pillars. Up ahead, a man

made Stonehenge from mufflers,
each piece salvaged and dragged like a plow.
See: I know. There is no need to hold my arm

tighter around the turns, though really,
I wouldn't mind. How lucky I am for your touch
steadying my shaky sugars, my pissing all night,

my body at war with my body.
It is not magic, I think, that wakes you
to rescue me, because the firemen,

the firemen in our apartment startled me
more than the need for them.
How lucky I am, I say, for your body,

how it awakens on this road,
how it never wavers.
Your hand on my thigh, long enough

to be damp, falls asleep, so you shake it.
Cars pass steadily in groups
going the other way.

STOPPING FOR DIRECTIONS

When I stopped for directions we argued. The man
in glasses behind the counter rose, said, *from here,*
pointing at a small spot on the map, black as night,
follow the fork. He traced a line on the map too
many times, explaining it leads toward nothing,
tall ponderosas, rabid dogs, and a stream, *one-*

two feet deep. Browns and rainbows weave there, one
around another. Yesterday, he said, a young man
hooked ten in an hour. Said they'd hit anything—
folded gum wrappers, small kernels of corn. *Out here,*
he said, *everyone is desperate.* There were two
pictures on the register: a cabin at night,

a fire engulfing that cabin, turning the night
almost day bright. He said he lost everything—once.
His wife, an autographed Ty Cobb baseball, his two
leopard cats, a bloodhound too senile to help the man,
too dumb too, to smell the burning sofa or hear
his wife, her screams returning back to the nothing

they were born from. He said he remembers nothing
that day gave. Only the quiet before the night
gives into itself. He hears
in dreams his dog barking up the wrong tree, no one
there except the trees and a beautiful woman
too lovely for his wife, *too lovely,* he said, *too*

damn lovely. He said it happens, regular, twice
each week. The doctors say, *sorry, there is nothing
to do.* He must go on living as he must. *Man,
it's easy,* he said, *keep driving straight through the night.*
I looked back at the map trying to find the one
line he traced with his finger. *Right here?*

I asked, trying to act dumb, as if I couldn't hear
misery, his footsteps, his loud breathing, his two
cats frantically clawing through the screen or his one
dog still digging holes in his dreams. There is something
to turn up: photographs of a cabin at night,
pictures of a woman standing next to a man.

Old man, out here, unlike you, I can say nothing.
Tonight we are two clouds hovering in the sky—
one swiftly a bluebird, the other a crouched man.

THE CIRCUS

The circus started red and then was gone,
a hopeless lover on the rail of a bridge,
maybe happy to be walking,
or maybe spying above the pine tree line
for an obscure word for star. A man on a black stage

is dragged into the rafters. He looks scared.
Suddenly the floor turns
to water. Everyone is wet. The acrobat in a leotard
dips from a swing into the blue floor and comes back
alive, as if recalling shedding her clothes

by oaks with a boy, not even her age, wading waist deep
in the night's frigid water. We know nothing
but expectation clapping at love
hanging from a rope. We think this might turn
to a love story because so often it does.

The man in the rafters has returned to fend off
a hunchback in a knit cap. The hunchback
must think this scene has played itself
for years in his dreams. Men and women in body suits
appear from the depths and somersault through air.

The floor moves to a rhythm all its own.
My girlfriend, who also reappears, snatches my hand
and whispers, *thank you,* but there is nothing I can do.
I've lost myself before.

WANTING

Her dog won't stop barking at bicycles,
chasing after the quick legs of people
pedaling them. Because he will get hit
she wants him to stop
being that boy, she says, she outgrew
at thirteen. She wants to quit
anticipating disaster.

She wants him to stop
smelling piles of shit on the pavement,
stop eating leaves, plastic straws,
bits of birds and frogs.

She wants him to stop choosing the things
that shouldn't be chosen.

He reminds her of her past
boyfriends, their preference to pee outside,
going handless they'd say,
while suggesting she hold it.

She thinks she wants something,
the ability to pee freely
or walk the streets alone
without a cell phone or a key
gripped tightly between her knuckles.

She wants the men in her life
to leave less of a mess, to choose
the marks they make more carefully.

She wants music before sex
and her last boyfriend's slow hand
to skip over the small bulge of her belly.
She wants him to quit complaining
about the dog's jingly collar
and the way she stays the same
like the morning train
always announcing the morning.

DELIVERING THE WORD

When you unlock your body
from mine the air-conditioned air
stutters in. It makes me think
there must be a sign for everything:
our chance meeting,
the way one can, if given time,
miss anything—

if given time, even the ring-a-ding
of an ice cream truck.

So when I start in
about signs: how the flower pattern
on your dinner plates matches my parents',
your name's relation to the stars,
the hours we spend
cuddled on the couch watching TV,
quick as a flick of your lighter,
you deliver it: *never mind.*

LOSING

Behind the iron trellis is where I found him,
searching the burnt brown ground

for a small sparkle, the hint of something shining steel.
His wife was going to kill him,

he said, in a manner which meant his meaning
was more serious than true. He only threw the ball

and before he knew his wedding ring flew from his finger
in a direction even God, he was sure, was unsure about.

The porch light lit small
stretches of the yard; it lit low limbs of the citrus;

it lit John, there beneath it, parting
the blades of grass with his hands until his hands

became lost, incapable of doing anything,
even separating.

SONG FOR THE OTHER SIDE

The reason for my wakefulness is not
her voice through the phone,
nor the difference in sound
between snowy egret and egret

swooping down from the clouds
more sure of itself than Moses.
It isn't even the sounds of night
rubbing together like socked feet.

On every driveway, posted
to the gate or stapled to a tree,
Keep Out. A few, *Trespassers*
Will Be Shot. So, how can I sleep

in this desperately singular sensation
of pine tree line, road,
car driving with its headlights on
two hours too early,

a small cloud, chimney smoke?
On the phone when she said, *it hurts*
when you let go, I believed
her voice fully burning,

a bottom log in the fireplace.
I believed I'd walk away more myself
than when I walked in.
I believed that chimney

would always be chimney, river
river, and the difference between
hurting and *missing,* only the leaf
we are free to watch fall.

THE ABORTION

I'm the type of guy that wonders
why blackbirds are called blackbirds;
bluebirds are called jays; redbirds,
cardinals; and why none eats the wind
toppled grapefruit around my tree.

I'm the type of guy that wonders
how to keep them
from the garden, even though I know,
the peas and the carrots refuse to take,
they refuse to take and grow.

I'm the type that thinks things
usually change
overnight: snow fall, leaf color,
a fever, a darkened room
after a fight.

I'm the guy that cries
during movies; that empties his pockets
down a brown glass jar;
that doesn't wait thirty minutes
between eating and swimming and believes,
no matter what most mothers say,
a cramp can't cause a drowning.

I'm the type of guy that leaves
ten minutes too early to appointments;
all yellow stains on snow alone;
with no one to name me
like I did my father.

ECLIPSE

We argue about furniture and the day empties.
The hair dryer's long wail doesn't stop
and she hums songs loud enough for me to hear.

On the other side of the fence, children walk
the football field for exercise;
their paths turn the grass into mud.

She looks back at me as if I were her coffee cup,
as if I were the one
worth setting down then leaving, and leaving

was nothing but one foot in front of the other,
left, right, left around the lake
that never completely freezes, past a duck

who has flown away; as if leaving was the room
inside a room
where the mood darkens when I enter.

As I woke to the news
which she watched in passing, putting on eye liner
and jarring the too big bed with her knee each time she left

the closet, saying *shit,* the weatherwoman pointed
to a whirling whiteness above Illinois, Michigan, Indiana,
and Ohio and said, *No moon*

for the Midwest tonight. One more good reason to live
in the desert. And I agreed and smiled and thought, *what else*
might be this good: the woman who didn't love me back

turning into the woman who did. The way the light can shine,
if I let it, into my room. It must be the calico cat
the realtor called Worthless, so I call Worthless,

who waits to leap from the compost pile
like fire from a match to scare me, to scare the trash bag
right out of me, as it falls in rocks from my hand;

who waits each morning for something small to eat,
like the squirrel, who once plucked her red
fuck-me bra from the clothesline and ate it,

the way time does at a body that bulges and bends.
We must ask ourselves, at times like these, questions:
how did we get here,

in a house next to a house next to a house, and why cow
over buffalo? And when she doesn't answer,
I know there is nothing left of us

but cordial phone calls,
a reservation for dinner, Ethiopian, where we'll wonder
if they really eat this well, where we'll split the bill,

a bottle of too sweet white wine because we have to,
to remember and end and forget all at once,
the days into months, the distance time travels from *a* to *b*,

from *m* to *e*, doubled and then squared
like a child's insult when time was the digital tick
of a watch, the last lit lamppost . . .

Where is her voice now? Rummaging through the refrigerator
I suppose, getting more and more angry that the leftovers
are no longer left. I could call her name

and she'd return to the foot of the bed,
her hand resting on her hip, her hair curled at the tips,
and I'd forget everything that I ever wanted

from her besides sex.
I'd forget the peeling metal porch rail,
the weeds growing through the cracks in the sidewalk

where I fertilized in rows, missing them,
the sun glare on the weatherwoman's face.
I'd forget about heaven and hell

and the moon's eclipse. But, I'd still ask if she wanted to see it,
to set up a couple of chairs or a blanket
on the grass, set up a life outside our life, if just for a second,

if just for the time it takes the sun to cover the moon
or the moon to cover the sun, which might take only a minute
or maybe, tonight, all night.

MISSING

People in the city were dying. Even you, my love. I began to cry. My tears were red but not blood. There was no room in the inn, in our garage, in the rusted two-toned '85 Oldsmobile my father gave me at sixteen. I took you to the curb. The crickets thanked me with their legs and said *vacancy* to dark places, turning themselves on and off. Do not blame me for the inconsistencies in this life—broken halos of moon, full halos of moon, no moon, a streetlight, and you, bug, underneath it dead.

II

POSTCARDS I SHOULD
SEND TO YOU

Neither the book in my lap
nor the two mesquites outside,
bowing in—then back—
their roots planning their stay
long before me, could tell
what love was supposed to be
while I stared out the window,
searching for something to happen
anytime now.

The moon is up again, half covered
in clouds coming down the Big Horns.
A single car cares nothing
for two lovers, drunk and lifting
each other's shirts while dancing
in muddy garage light across the street.

Tonight, silence has taken many forms.
In the bedroom, she lies naked,
spooning the pillow in my place.

*

Whatever the road leading you here,
you are here and we are alone.
Almost unnatural, the way we talk
out our lives to live them.

Once a woman and I made promises
and love in every state
between Michigan and Arizona.
Once in the car, once in a patch
of pines that grew crooked
and out of place, once I thought I was romantic,
taking her to the roof in the rain.

Now, if she asked about love, I'd say
I believe we made a mark.
However insignificant the things we build,
we build the thing.
We build and destroy, build and keep,
build and give away our streets.

*

Whatever the road that leaves you here,
we are alone on the coast of nowhere
past Midland and Saginaw, Hell and Hope
where the old factory stacks stop and rest.

The neighbor boy takes pot shots at the elm
squirrel. The squirrel leaps unsteady,
branch to branch. Somehow, I take it all in
and the window elbows it all back out.

Used to be the fourth grade boys would run
to the swings, dodge Mrs. Wall and stand in circles
in the sand. They would hunch over, pull the sand
into two large breasts and draw a face, with smile.

Each in turn, they rocked back and forth
until they flew, more awkward than a failing kite,
arms outstretched, embracing something
their bodies didn't fit.

They would land on their bellies
between the sand girl's tits, jump upright,
build the mounds back up, a line of boys,
working together, over and over again.

*

I've seen her here before
on Route 52, past the fairgrounds
where last night a man got crushed
like a pop can between a junked-up Ford
and Chevy in the demolition derby.

She stands in the gravel shoulder
behind a sweet corn cart
waving an American flag and a sign,
10 Ears For A Buck.

Her dress is a blue familiar
only to dreams or a lousy B movie
where voices trail actions
as fireworks trail thunder.

Today it is all the same.
Behind her are fields of emptiness
and her father is already stuck
like Motown in a bar.

THE WINTER OF 1990

We hid behind a pine tree
waiting, sometimes for hours,
crouched low to the ground,

our bodies tangled in its limbs.
We cannonaded piles of ice balls,
each one dipped in a bucket of water

then set out to freeze,
hard as algebra.
They were indestructible.

Each time we threw them
with the wind-up and release
they left strawberry bruises on our chests.

One of us always cried.
If it snowed, we started early
faking paths through the field

so our tracks were scattered and distant.
We knew each other's flight
by shoe size, and the field

better than our bodies.
It all started the spring before,
launching over-ripe apples

that splattered on a windshield.
Sometimes we forgot
the cars and their headlights,

their quick passings, long
empty trains to the bay.
Sometimes we chickened out,

missing on purpose,
throwing the ice ball too late.
It was our way—the waiting,

the snow in the field.
Whatever we knew we knew.
Some nights passed quick and dark

and we fought, choking each other
face down in the snow.
Some nights no cars at all.

Some nights a door opened.
A dog barked from behind a fence.
It recognized nothing.

Once, when I was not there,
they threw a snowball and hit a car
dead on. They said they got a good look—

a man going down
on another man. And I wonder, right now,
if my friends remember this.

Some gave chase. I know it.
Some sat frozen,
scared as deer.

UNKNOWN GRANDFATHER, 1997

After reading about Sarajevo and the bombs
exploding against dark roof tiles, lies
tearing away from other lies,
it seems natural, doesn't it, to think of death?

In a small Jewish cemetery, children play games,
striking ripe sycamore pods that burst
on contact with a stick, then sprint grave to grave
as if history had a head start.

In the trees, birds cry.
Everything, save the season, is the same.
Some grandfather's headstone is empty of rocks.
Once, I carried a pebble in my pocket
from Nice to Detroit and placed it,
gray as winter, on my desk.

I wanted to think bombs don't drop
on target, that all planes are manned by my friends,
like Dax, who wanted out
and fell backward from a rising Apache.
Sometimes the moon is a flat stone.
Sometimes it is heavy and falling.

The children leave their games in the grass.
First, over their shoulders, night descends.
Elms and pines and layers of sky disappear
over the empty gravestone
love could not save from memory.

FROM THAT DISTANCE
for my brother

Out of the frozen blue, you called
across the field. From my blind,
from that distance, I thought you a deer

and lifted the barrel butt.
Each step over snow snapped.
Without sounding a shot

you broke through thin ice
where in summers
we sat watching minnows go,

the way they didn't stop swimming,
the way they fought the current
just to stay where they were,

under shadows of old brown stones.
Sam, after all these winters
I still haven't asked

what it was you wanted.
Tonight, in this desert, the first monsoons.
The wind pushes a linebacker

from Heritage High under my tin
covered parking spot. It lifts
and crashes. These are not our storms.

These are not those times
on the columned porch, shucking corn,
throwing hair and skin in the bag between us,

waiting for that one loud crash
of thunder, for that one strike of an infinite
moving-on to a place without us.

MY BROTHER MET LOU FERRIGNO
OUTSIDE A HAUNTED HOUSE

And it was good, tasteful, the way he sat
almost alone, speaking to my brother as a brother:
a hug, exchanges of money, a photo to remember him
big and strong and green crashing through a wall.
There was no line—no one else came to see him.
It seemed the end to all ends was actually here—
a haunted house in October, in weather
unseasonably warm, in a hug and a souvenir picture.
I don't know if they talked TV,
baseball, or the way mountains in this town
look more like red camels than mountains.
Children scurried from the haunted house EXIT like roaches
and I remembered the only true way out
is at the end, past the masked high school boys,
secretly high, secretly laughing and in love
with the girls who run straight through the plastic-net wall
of the make-shift haunted house like Lou himself did.
All I know is it was a long time before my brother turned to leave
Lou sitting there like a rock.

TATTOO

When I turned sixteen and found my license
read '74 not '79, Peanut drove for the twelve pack
we drank too quickly at the drainage creek,
throwing our empties at the robins in the trees,
which would take off, in panic, and return,
take off and then return.

It was a game the birds knew. Soon we would leave,
soon the rotting apple of the sky would darken.
And when it did, we did.
We walked two blocks to the tattoo shop.
We flipped pages of anchors,
of anchors and waves, of big anchors splashing

like a whale's tail before a face appeared, a demon with a tongue
that curled. I thought I was living. A car, no curfew,
no black eye, and a buzz.
I wanted to be crazy, not end up like my father
or brothers or friends who had grown roots
too long in a town surrounded

by streams. Now, we're no different, them
and me. Our imperfections. There is a fiery face
on my leg I see before bed, a face on my leg
not mine. And I remember my father
placing his soft hand over it, pleading
how's it come off, how's it come off?

ACCIDENT AT THE CHOCOLATE FESTIVAL

From the woman falling over
a hard hollow sound
rises from the pavement, an open

slap against the belly
of a watermelon. From the crowd
too stunned to help,

a young woman and child
walk by passing back
and forth pieces of a funnel cake.

In my awkwardness,
I fidget toward her,
but she is gone

confusing me for a man
named Joe. I nod.
Her friend runs

circles around us.
The crowd keeps moving.
A boy walks

a white marionette bear
in short spasms
down the sidewalk.

THE LUNCH LADY USES
BAD LANGUAGE

Martha made grilled cheese
on the griddle and the steam
made her hair fall.
When Martha was cold,
under her apron
she wore her son's bowling jacket,
his name embroidered on its back
so we saw *Steve* instead.

Sometimes staring in surprise
at *Steve* we'd see Martha more,
the lines of her underwear,
her breasts when the air was hot
and thick and stuck to her body.

Once, when she saw us looking
she grabbed her chest and said,
*in Poland ants grow big
as potatoes.* Then she shook
her breasts with her hands
so her breasts themselves
seemed like hands, hands
holding potatoes.

That was the way she talked,
always in metaphors,
always with loud hands—

her boss was a rat, her son
a baboon, the weather, hell.
Her hands spoke
the only language we understood.

III

WHEN THE RADIO SCARES
THE ROADRUNNERS

A woman in a wheelchair next door
fidgets the porch radio into speech.
Two roadrunners startle
from the dried-up ditch.
Her black lab barks.

The roadrunners, downhill now,
look for food. The woman hums
along to a song my mother adored.

And when she turns the radio off
life itself seems to quiet so much
that if it sneaks up,
touches my shoulder,
I'd think for the moment
nothing is there.

DAY OF THE DEAD

*Each year on November 2, as the Monarch butterfly
arrives, thousands of people celebrate. This day-long
ritual, which includes parades, picnics in cemeteries,
and altars set up in the home, is an ancient festivity
that joyfully celebrates the dead.*

The street is suddenly loud.
Puppets share wine. A dog dressed
in a red gown growls.

Although there are children
they are not scared, like me.
They see skeletons come back alive
beating pots with wooden spoons.

Death is like that today:
a dark street night descends upon.

At the bus station
a dead priest waves his hand,
an upside down cross against his chest.
Somehow these strangers from Bisbee,
Nogales and Tombstone
know to join us. They can hear the drum,
that voice almost of prayer.

PROCESSION OF THE DEAD

A boy can't hold it
and pisses behind a dark dumpster
then runs down the street
to catch the dead
who have passed him by.

A girl, about twenty, dressed
like a whore has her own
procession following closely behind,
watching her ass through little
spilling moons of fishnet.

She whispers to her friend
and they giggle, knowing the dreams
of the living are following them.

RALLY OF THE DEAD

There is nothing here.
I have no picture
of the old Indianapolis farm.
All I do have, Grandma,
is your late arrival, complaining of car noises
and the road-kill deer on the interstate.

When my father looked under the hood
you made us pile in,
drive in circles around the block.

All I have now, Grandma,
is the knowledge that nothing was wrong.
Each year the sycamore on the corner
changes its color.

SLEEP

It finished
but never left.

It was a relative
in the bedroom

between the bathroom and kitchen.

The first noise is nothing—
a toilet seat

smashing down, water
filling the pipes,
a cat at the door.

But, in the yard, the wind,
that last performer,

gathers around
like a group of boys

until it becomes no more
than what it is—

a dance, falling pinecones,
blown stones.

BEFORE BREAKFAST

A family, I think, of small mule
deer has taken my shoe

beside the door
in haste. Suddenly as if nature

took the time for this—
the wind blew dust

blanketing a man with groceries.

THE THREE TABLES OF CHRIST

after Scorsese

I sit drunk
waiting my turn.

I can't help
but stare—
a young girl, her dark

pubic hair.

*

I wake to the silence
no longer mine,

as if waking outside,
watching a woman

birthing a cloud.

*

There is no place in bed.
There are no goblins in the closet.

No arm disappearing in the shower.

Still, a little of her remains.

It is paper hitting doors,
the morning.

THE IRIDESCENT PALO VERDE
UNDER A NEW MOON

Tonight there is no bone,
no hip, no mouth:

only the slip of your shoulder into sleep
folds night inside itself.

Between the diamond
of your legs upon mine

we are found, admiring
the moon's shadow.

If it were easy to lay
flowers down in desert wind,

at the base of your body,
I would.

But what if God continues
playing God, if the dove,

exhausted, drops again
into your branched hair?

Would we come here
through wave after wave

of indifference:
sky, water, sky

for a single branch
dried dead?

CANDLE

It wants existence in flame, lengthening breasts, until it burns star into star, autumn to winter, all alight with firmament—all heavy and falling. At a café in Place Bellecour it leapt like a mime imitating a small boy sucking his thumb asleep on his father's shoulders. Yesterday it said, *stop fucking around and get to the point.* Today it is awkward and selfish, smiling at a girl who stands searching for her underwear on the floor. It exhausts itself—says to her, look again.

WHEN YOU ASK

You can find the country's map
on the back of a hand
held out in front of a body—
in every pore, each shattered knuckle.

The middle finger is the long slab
stretch of I-75. Above it, cold
Canadian air bites. Either way,
empty air around the hand
is cold water,

and to flip the map is to find its pulse,
a willow that hangs limp
all the days and nights without light
except for a streetlamp, a table lamp,

the sudden
candle light leap of salmon,
right out of themselves,
when winter ends with thaw.

BEFORE GOD MADE GOOD

It is true, what they said, a crow can call
a soul into answer.
It is true. Before day there was darkness
so vast and unimaginable
our outspread arms were our eyes,
the white cataract of a stubbed finger.

Those days the wind sifting
the fallen leaves didn't console us, didn't tell us
anything about ourselves except this
insistent need for warmth. And we liked it,

huddling together, holding our arms
up to each other, greeting
the old fashioned way,
somewhere between a hug and a kiss,
no matter what sex
we wanted each other to be.

We were what we wanted.

MISSING CITY 1

The city has a name
which has forgotten me.
There, two men live, each
hoping to fill the missing part
of the other. They tend to dream
the same hyacinth dream.

There is an asylum on a hill
in the city which guards it.
I almost remember the story—
a man runs mad
to the corner of two streets
shaded by pines.

Once there and not there,
all at once, he climbs a light pole
and makes a nest,
perched, now flipping pages
of an old paperback.

After an hour a patrol stops
and calls to him. Birds worth naming
fly V then broken V
like white ribbons.

They said he's done this before.

MISSING CITY 2

There is an absence in the heart—
rotini boils in a pot

without water. Dinner will eat
itself under the supper table.

There is no grace.

Afterwards, our husband and wife
wash dishes that were left for weeks

by someone neither has ever seen.

It is like that here—
dumb and blind with snow.

The night never expects night to end,
like winter dragging itself

into late May fields. In the plaza,
two men sit at a table and drink dark beer.

From another town
music pours over the far hills in horizons.

MISSING CITY 3

There is a vault under the asylum
saving the remnants of the city.

Mice roam like gods under a dark
cracked sky devouring anything—

the rookie Mickey Mantle, an incisor
tucked in a little pocket inside a little pillow—

anything worth anything but still remaining—
a love note written from the sane

to the insane, neither one knowing
what damages the other most,

a pocket magnifying scope, half-filled
tax returns, photographs of a father

standing short and proud by a cornfield.
There are things no one wants to dig up.

Trust me. I'm not telling you
the mice are as big as cats.

MISSING CITY 4

The city is full. It is late August
and the streets will disappear like romance,
everything but the clouds heading south
for the cold. If we could stop them,
we would. Hill pines surrounding
the asylum are winded and ready
to topple with a touch.

A man and woman walk hand in hand
through bad light,
home. He looks for love
like keys in his pocket. We have all loved
poorly. Along the street the bars
and their neon signs glow open.

The streets have names no one
here can pronounce. Some words
mean other things, some,
just what they are.

IV

WHAT'S WRONG WITH BEING HUMAN

I lived two houses down a dead end street.
When the river ran rough
we checked our basements.
We called to each other to help.
We hauled boxes up
from the dark like large fish.

When Mary or Mark or Helen died,
little by little,
we all did. We sent flowers.
The street took to looking
like a Cadillac. It grew bolder.
It grew rosy cheeks.

When Jack repainted, John
repainted, and the painters
ate lunch on the roof.

We said *it looks nice,*
nodding at our mailboxes.
We waved while shoveling snow
off the walkway no one walked
but the dogs and our manic-depressive mailman.

When we wanted an egg or a glass
of milk we drove to the store.
We stared out our windows.
Our children grew without parents.
We grew into speaking without words.

We thought our reflections
in the lamplight were only there
out of loyalty, and, if given
a chance, would run
like Mrs. Eddie's dead son
naked, through trees.

THE DUET

1.

A duet on the radio pleads to end
each day in song. If I had the choice,
my song would be quiet,
a little twang,
a trill when the voice hops up.

I'd sing a story you might know:
two kids, a brother and a brother,
tossing baseballs over the roofs of passing cars.
There'd be love enough to have one boy

sing to the redhead
on the bottom branch of a maple,
and without knowing it
he'd hum the song all wrong.

A boy gone the way of other boys,
stealing silver from his sister's jewelry box.
There'd be a fight with elbows and words,
a boy watching a girl walk away.

2.

There'd be a place to drive.
The boy there, in his pockets jingles

the night blind with moon.
The boy sings to a girl

even though his song sounds all wrong.
The song makes a street

she'd turned to for fifteen years
seem like a street she'd turned to in error.

To listen closer, she'd roll up the wind
in the window, tell him, drive the car in circles.

She wanted his song to touch her
the way a lip touches lip.

If she had the choice,
she'd want her song to be that quiet.

MONSOON MOVING ANTIQUITY
TO TUCSON

I sweat like windows on a city bus,
my hands move when I speak, my nose is nothing
more than a button, and when I walk, I sweat.

It's July, too hot for sparrows to sweep
air into breezes, and if the air somehow stirs,
it's hot as a hair dryer. On the way to Tucson,

behind row after row of pistachio trees,
a graveyard of airplanes, each boarded with plywood.
They sit yawning at the mountains.

Each year more planes are grounded, left
for dead. Through the hazy heat of midday,
rocks ripple. The planes seem troubled,
each hiding its tail behind the other.

Even awake and driving, I feel a need to end
my shift, like the man in the Mobil, who watched
crickets swarm in thousands down the candy aisle.

A HOUSE PAINTER, A LOVE SONG

She lived three townhouses down
with a woman too redheaded to be her mother
and her brother, who played basketball and peed in the
        chokeberry
that hadn't flowered in three years.
The chokeberry, management said, started growing
before they did, which makes it a worry
the way an ache in the hip means rain.

The girl sits on her back porch, unsuspicious,
by the chokeberry, most mornings,
watching the sun raise shadows
of houses from the fresh geranium-filled dirt.

I watched her while she watched the morning,
her brother, the ball bouncing awkwardly
left or right off rocks.
When she went indoors
I went to work, painting
the way absent-minded men do, recklessly
toward shade, the gutters, clogged heavy by the fat,
brown leaves. What I learned was unavoidable.

At first it was no rhythm, no fun.
The brush, a baby spilling on itself.
I dropped Meridian Rose on a lawn elf.
I couldn't paint a window
without taping the whole frame.
If I had wings I would paint better.

I thought, how can painters paint?
How can straight lines hold two disparate things
together and at the same time be nothing?
My hands thought constantly
about playing her thighs
the way she played the piano, each afternoon.
I looked at her through walls,
staring at piano keys like a shadow
of a shadow at 4:30 in the morning.
When does the hand stop from its obligations?

I JUST CALLED TO SAY

Each night I'd dream she'd wait a while in silence,
letting the words of the song or the sound of my voice
carry a current that swept over the roof top,
through the empty arms of the sycamore.
She lived two blocks away, and, in eighth grade,
I thought Stevie Wonder had as good a shot as any
at getting me laid. All I had to do was pick up the phone
and sing a song about picking up a phone.
I'd play the way the song would sound in my head.
I'd be singing, nailing notes, imagining the girl
I loved loving every minute of it.
She'd wait there, as I said, in silence, twirling
stray strands of her hair around her finger,
motioning with her free hand to her friends,
for them to come over and listen.
I thought that this was the way to win
her heart. For once, I could be somebody
who knew how to woo a girl
into love and sex, so it could come, and come
to me, naturally. When I told my brother my plan
he called me a pussy and said I sang like shit.
Still, I thought, somehow, someway, I could be the one
so many boys talked about:
tougher than Tommy's fifth grade quiz
when he herded us into the last stall of the boy's bathroom
and showed us a picture of a bent
over bare woman's ass, and asked, which hole

was which. And although I knew I'd never be Tommy,
that when I answered him wrong
it would follow me for life, although I knew
my friends would taunt me, I thought
that this song and the way I could sing it
could make a girl make me a man.
But now, it seems, no one laughs
at the way we want love. Just last week
when I returned the last stack of my ex's cds,
no one laughed when
it took three turns around the block to pull in.

TODAY IS GARAGE SALE DAY

After a night of wind, he wakes
to the sound of his father's voice
complaining about the roof,
how it leaks down the edge of the chimney.
He can picture his father standing there,
next to the elk head he hung
last November, pointing at the yellow rings
forming fourteen feet above them.

Sleepy eyed, he slips on
the only rubber soled boots he can find
and opens the door. In front of him,
overnight, the wind broke the aspen
and the way it has fallen
face-first against the fence
is enough work for weeks.
His wife, already in and out of the shower,
has slapped his ass twice.
By now, he figures she's circling
the classifieds, she's sipping some coffee.
By now, she's drawing a map.

He knows her excitement lies in the finding
of things unexpected, like the tattoo
hidden on his right thigh.
Last month alone, she bought a sea
shelled soap dish, a French press,
a plastic lemonade pitcher and matching glasses

with stenciled-on ducks. Perfect,
she said, for summer, for kids and a pool.

He knows today will be no holiday.
He will spend his time surveying tools.
There will be a banged-up skill saw, a ratchet set
missing most of its sockets.
There will be little homemade grab bags
filled with mismatched screws and nails.

He will joke about the stupidity of strangers
trying to sell underwear for a nickel,
and remember, how once, she picked a pair
from a crumpled, cardboard U-Haul box
and lifted them to his waist.

He laughed, not at the scene: them,
stuck on a Saturday, scanning knick-knacks
on card tables in cleaned up,
respectable garages, garages without spiders
crawling up the corners, flat-tired bikes
dangling down from hooks, or bags of trash
piled on a child's red wagon; he laughed
at the word she chose, how she said *panty,*
instead of underwear; he laughed at how
emasculated it made him feel, watching her
throw the panties back in the box.

But today could be a good garage sale day.
The mailman has come early, parking
his truck with two tires on the curb.
His wife, any minute, will walk outside
holding her checkbook, her ID, and folding the map
she made into quarters. He knows
when they leave the last garage
he will get to pick the place for lunch.
He will carry whatever she holds
in her hands at the time, even lace five cent panties,
and on the way to the car he will offer
a gift of certainty.
He will offer her his hand.

SUNDAYS AT SUNSET

My love is gone
tending a man in a wheelchair.
In the first fifteen minutes
she told me she saw his cock,
limp and stricken.

Here, a couple watching the band
called the river a lake. The mariachis
are playing their final song in Spanish.
Two men are lying on a blanket,

drinking red wine from crystal.
One turns to smile, then the other smiles
and I smile, though they take
no notice.

The men on stage sway
to a rhythm I cannot dream,
all silver and sparkling.

PHOTOGRAPH OF THE GRAND CANYON
HANGING IN A REST AREA ON I-10

Around you, winter's quick kick of wind
arouses a small patch of leaves.
Out of the canyon come flying voices of birds
we can't see, wings we can't hear.
Detachment sounds like that, I think, an eagle
high over the palo verde.

The trail leans forward in front of us
until it switches back around large sandstone rocks.
The edge, always much closer
than it appears. I am nervous and sing songs
in my head. There is nothing but time
and its narrowing of a life
in this desert. You keep quiet, understanding
how night grows steep.

At a clearing, out of tired necessity, we stop
and lie down on our bellies.
In a dream things could be different—
I become sick and you help me
to my feet, carrying me, scraping your legs
along the prickly pear. Anything could happen:

rocks fall, fires burn, a boy in Katmandu
crawls on his stomach for fifty miles,
eyes averted from the sky so blue

only a god feels fit to live in it.
In dream, image is simple—an ocean swallows
northern California, alligators tear off
my right foot, you haul me from this mountain
out of a death spin.

SPEAKING TO EACH OTHER THE WAY
WE SPEAK TO FRIENDS

I've never understood the ratios,
tall to short, soda to rum.
The bartender has a gut
larger than my own,
a remark by time itself
on the hours it took to get here.

He asks not about the day or score.
Our team walking away with their hats raised
is a long shot
we continue to hope for.

We both know baseball, watch it
long past the lights light up.
We watch boys turn
inside themselves when a pitch pushes in.

We only differ now in the way we stand ready,
his hands on his belly,
mine on my knees.

When he asks, *what'll it be?*
all I know is I want to be again
a player with bat and ball,
feel the need to sail out flies,
sail them out to anyone in the grass who'll snag them.

So, when I motion with my hands
a tall, he knows my count exactly.

THE MESSENGER
for John Espinoza

I think the bird that shit on your shoulder is not a messenger of God
as you said, but only a bird, a bird that chose the tree above us.
But, also as you said, what if the bird was racist?
It could have landed on that branch spotting a darker man.
I'd have to think the opposite though.
I'd have to think that sometimes birds hide too
behind laughter. They must want. They must need to ride
a bike or drive 65 in a car without wind
smearing tears to their faces. The question is then
was it bliss or hate that the bird felt for you.
Was it a joke, the way we are all jokes to someone else as they talk
sweetly in bed? What difference John,
the way we get shit on ourselves?
It is bound to happen. We are bound to the earth
just as birds are bound to sky.
Sometimes what we think is soaring is actually
a hell of a lot of work.

IF PRACTICE MADE PERFECT

The neighbor's child outside could sink
his three point shot, the moon
could make any man more darling,
and those people constantly calling
on the phone during dinner
could draw us forth.
If practice made perfect
there'd be no dicks caught in zippers,
no stumbling on stairs,
no mischievous cat meowing
morning into light, no girl
in my car coming home from the bar
rubbing her softest spots
while I watch, swerve, hit
two curbs. There'd be no wind
in the window, no rare cool breeze.
If practice made perfect
there'd be no deadening drops
of sugar in my blood, no way
to say through my panic, my needs.
If practice made perfect
there'd be no sound lovelier
than the word used to describe it,
no road not mapped,
no river worth more than its water.

OUR LAST EVENING, AFTER LAUNCHING FROM THE BOTTOM OF THE HOOVER DAM

for John, David and Lee

We play cards to drink
quicker than we would on our own.
The dealer'd say *drop*
and we'd slap the single card,
sweat-stuck against our foreheads,
down on the Coleman cooler
we brought to keep ice ice
five full days.

Now, after two, it all
went to water
warm enough to fish through in darkness.

The four women sit back behind us,
slouched in their seats
along the river's night rise,
and having made a small circle, talk
about the talk of us men.

How decency doesn't matter
on vacation; how nakedness is still
a surprise like the man in the hot spring,
completely hairless,
tucking his uncircumcised penis
between his legs and waving

with a nod while we walked
through the pools of thigh high water;
how screwed those young couples
we saw lugging kids.

No matter what
when someone clears the cards,
lifts the beach-stained lid,
he pulls out two. We refuse to believe
the other is done playing
so we wait to the end
drinking and cheering whatever happens,
and what little life we have left
we will spend.

NOTES & ACKNOWLEDGMENTS

Eternal thanks to Norman, Beckian, Tito, Cynthia and Karla for their friendship, support and guidance, which has been instrumental in the making of this book. I want to thank K, B, N, and J who listened to these poems literally hundreds of times.

The author is grateful for a fellowship from the Virginia G. Piper Center for Creative Writing, which allowed me time to finish the book.

Acknowledgment to the editors of the following publications, in which certain poems first appeared, sometimes in earlier versions:

42Opus: "The Duet," "Our Last Evening, After Launching from the Bottom of the Hoover Dam"

The Drunken Boat: "If Practice Made Perfect," "What's Wrong With Being Human," "Before God Made Good"

Fugue: "The Messenger"

Gulf Coast: "My Brother Met Lou Ferrigno Outside a Haunted House"

Indiana Review: "Missing"

Meridian: "I Just Called to Say"

Paradigm: "Missing City 1," "Missing City 2," "Missing City 3," "Missing City 4"

Passages North: "Spectators Along the Interstate," "Stopping for Directions"

Prism International: "Tattoo"

Puerto Del Sol: "Wanting"

Rhino: "Eclipse"

Rosebud: "Iridescent Palo Verde Under A New Moon"

Sycamore Review: "After a Long Separation"

Verse Daily: "Spectators Along the Interstate"

Ausable Press is grateful to

The New York State Council on the Arts

The National Endowment for the Arts

The New York Community Trust

for their generous support.